Black State Cars

Black State Cars

Alan Jude Moore

salmonpoetry

Published in 2004 by
Salmon Publishing Ltd.,
Cliffs of Moher, County Clare, Ireland
Website: www.salmonpoetry.com
email: info@salmonpoetry.com

ISBN 1 903392 40 3

Cover artwork: *Chaiki* by Victor Aklomov, 1977. Reproduced with the kind
permission of the Moscow House of Photography.

Cover design & typesetting: Siobhán Hutson

Salmon Publishing gratefully acknowleges the
support of The Arts Council / An Chomhairle Ealaíon

Acknowledgments

Acknowledgement is due to the editors of the following in which a number of these poems first appeared:

Poetry Ireland Review, The Burning Bush, The Stinging Fly, Books Ireland, Ropes, West 47, The New Writer, Kestrel, The Glass Cherry, The Unknown Writer, The Colombia Review and *Jacobs Ladder.*

Contents

Shipping News

Ripples on the canal overturn and sink
a child's paper boat. A swan, poised,
floats by. (Or, the ghost of a swan).
Last night a tanker sank
off the coast of Buenos Aires.
Reuters promptly reported this,
via the shipping news: the child looking
for a stick to reach out across oceans,
to perform a mission of salvage. The swan
waiting for his lady to change direction.

Heading into darkness outside Athlone

Heading into darkness outside Athlone,
stolen segments of parchment, the landscape;
farms and various apparatus for hanging
names on scraps of people and places.
The roads and river look old, planted
beside an automated transportation depot.
Some horses stand mouths gaping open.
Likewise, after a hard night of drinking,
heading into darkness between Athlone and Moate;
battlefields, externalised historical centres.
Tiny pities of the aristocracy still roll down hills
to mingle with the smell
of bogwood and treacherous bog.
In rooms where no-one laughs,
(or has even come close to a tear for some time),
sentiment is wrapped in a paper bag
of title deeds and co-operative agreements.
Through cat's eyes, a service light or EXIT sign,
heading into darkness outside Athlone,
a city waits like a sentinel hung out to dry.
Seated nine rows down on a private coach,
heading into darkness outside Athlone.
History coils around my leg
and begs I believe the future scheme of things
is not decided by horses or men; insects
crawling up the window fall back down again.

Flowers have fallen on your shoulder

Flowers have fallen on your shoulder.
The colours make you look like an ornament,
a vessel you have neglected. Some people
you know question the stability of a petal
that comes close yet is never grounded.
But you imagine it reasonable, nature
in any shape or form compete with the dead
gull's beak, lying open on South Anne Street.

Flowers have fallen on your shoulder,
making you look the centre of something—
a stationary force or tiny galaxy.

Inland

I hear you swim in the river these days,
In picture postcard valleys, no salt in the air.
You moved inland, back to old stones and fields.
I think the seagulls know that something's gone on.
They dip sadly over our bricks and patches of grass,
Through the sunlight tangled in the cranes.
Bound to the place, torn and useless, but inescapable.
From this distance I can almost see you.
Your eyes clawing at my eyes. From that distance.
How you must have practiced all this time
To send a low sun fast into the morning,
Dripping grey mid-country light.
How you must have practiced all this time,
To tell me I did not learn to love you.

The Hook

Today there is no news on the streets.
They run only with a business, against which
silence is useless:
with a war between sides of whom nothing is spoken.
Within it we run marathons,
to keep in shape for the next one.
Like messengers without direction.

Today there is no news on the streets;
but basins full of reeking fish,
the dying slip across the dead.
We relay signals, to maintain the medium,
burn dead leaves to clear debris that blows
through the cracks; unnoticed until
the carbon frame is examined
and the skeleton exhumed.

Today there is no news
to say what damage might be done.
We do not need to be told or count the costs,
we hold the world on our shoulders
and bite like sharks at each new currency
cast from above.

In the style demanded by our silence,
we set fire to things, eradicate distance
and lunge forward like industrious athletes.
With a claw in our hands, we tell ourselves—
today there is no news on the streets,
we are as strong as the buildings we build;
with a hook in our mouths, we are like fish
landed in the dirt.

Impression

A craggy Beckett lookalike
Standing in the doorway
Of a restaurant
No more
No less
Your cigarette
Will fall from your lips
If you do not
Pay it more attention

Republic / Elegy

Each moment of your absence spells the future.
Old and bare, your absence should not grow.
But you were taught how to be imperial,
to always let roses sweeten the blow.
That I cannot find the words to make you stay
is an indication of all my power.
That you departed when you did is the bequest
of manners and a proper education.
It's clever you speak French and Spanish,
one language is often not enough.
Our language often fails us when we need it the most,
when roses are nothing
but remnants of old glory.

Hands held like swan's necks

Hands held, like swan's necks
entangled. Each other has a need,
hangs like a vulture, works in
on itself. Dirty grey newsprint
comes between them; seed
floats by. Feathers fall before
the naturally disappointed, perched
in parks like parakeets; beneath
shadows that swoop to the throat.
Traffic recalls these creatures,
more so than rivers or light,
to marching band time.

A hunger between them unspoken,
like bad news of any sort.

The Prisoner Speaks of a Woman

Her body moves in the vocabulary of shadows,
through the country between us, the time
I have plotted against us.
Her eyes cover ground like searchlights
across a landscape wounded by desire.
Her voice is raised to the language of distant dogs
beating through a pass as the moon gives way.
Her breasts like campfires
where the heart survives, secret and violent.
Lips like satellites of the canary and the rosebush.

The sun bleeding like a bullet hole
through the windows and the bars,
over graveyards and processions.

The Gallery

A bird singing in Archbishop Ryan park
That woman on the train was talking as if she knew you
Like it mattered
This morning has an arcade of sorrows
A rope of tears stretched by the sun
From the station to the movement
Of clerks and secretaries
Singing in the traffic

(Van Gogh would have been pleased with the bud
On that tree to the left
The way it's hung around for days waiting to flower)

The way it's been there forever

After Degas,

Dancers in Blue

One blue dancer adjusts her shoulder strap
as if no-one is looking.
The secretary in the office down the hall
does almost the same thing
each day before getting in the lift
and staring in the mirror.
Or during Lent,
taking the exit to the stairs;
making up her reflection in the window.

After Degas,

The Star

No scrolled head of a double bass
No friends
or choreographer
No paper shapes
behind her white body
and pinpoint red lips
In a white dress
flowers bleeding down the front
from her breast
It seems almost sincere
The slim leg
    twisted
    into position
The crown of Summer
piercing perfect skin
Her balance maintained
in the right hand corner
Painless
Waiting
for the curtain to fall

I do not remember

I do not remember how I held you,
now we are both broken free. I do not remember
those moments of freedom between us. And
I do not remember the slow death of our time,
stations washed in a little rain, hallways bleeding
history.
　　The sound of your heart has torn itself
from your breast and it wanders like a ghost
through houses where I lose myself. I have not
remembered our distances were changed.
　　The maps or the politics of states,
I do not recall what it was I pledged to, but something
has been betrayed. I do not remember all the words
that loved you. I tried to find them in windows
framing the body you grew without me. Now
flowers grow in our shadow, the evening calls
for silence and lamplight falls like a language
I do not understand.

Berlin

We have drifted like the scent of eyelashes from your pillow.
Again the world reveals itself
between the legs of distant women;
making love across the wall,
arm in arm, alone like stars
that fall and come to nothing.

Arm in arm, consumed by history;
like the communists of our childhood,
the fevered Bay of Pigs, Marx and Jesus.

So you tempt me with your mouth of glass,
the dance of light across your skin or the smell of your lover
from the night before. And I want you like a city
where there's always something worse to do.

Arm in arm, alone like stars, I hadn't slept for days;
heard gunshots in my dreams and holes appeared
from everywhere. Your teardrops cut my wrist,
made me something new but bruised;
something I could not believe in.

Arm in arm, alone and listening for the sound
of dogs and breaking wire.
The coloured screen still reveals
others like us will be found,
hiding in the ruins or crying at the bar,
falling down stairs or rolling up our notes
where the broken priests are sleeping and the Virgin's
image fades.

Arm in arm, alone like stars.
                              Berlin is against itself again.

And us our love is water
that does not know whether to be
a river or an ocean between us.

Stems from the wind and from the solar system,
from Heaven's gates, carved in the shape of tiger claws,
from Tridentine masks and the stock exchange—
leaves by the wind just the same.
Like ash or coke remain for a while
beneath our fingernails;
we will be blown into each other.

Arm in arm, our love is water.
Berlin is against itself again.

The Scavengers

A tightly pressed man eyes up his woman like a scrapbook.
An article encountered perhaps because
of a chance reorganisation of objects.
A button has come loose on his jacket,
he works to hide it from her field of vision,
while he maps a course of action across her skin;
tied to the secret operation of his need.
Pillars of promise and hope obscure them,
though they catch each other, like dust, now and again.
On the edge of her body, on the cliffs of her mouth;
he becomes a movement of scavengers gathering sand.
He looks at his lover like a collection of things,
achievements even, that have passed through his hands.

Letter from the Bridge

While waiting for you
carnival horses turned their tricks
and elephants waited
along the street
for something else to change.
Cheap displays
and Lebanese Red
passed for exhibition,
(before your naked shoulder
made my eyes spin wild
like rain drenched wheels).
Damp fireworks and the end
of cigarettes are all that's left.
Even after what we've done.
But you might have known
I'd call from that box
perched on the edge of the circus,
wearing your old discarded feathers;
like a brothel creeper or some other kind of hero.
(Above the parade children float by
tied to balloons and flags.
A flock of cranes creak
with all the grace of a nation
fleecing itself in the mirror).
Still you might have known
I'd have practiced what I'd say,
(the fortunes of others mean nothing to us).
You might have known:
a fistful of change
waving in a frightened tiger's face.
"The fortunes of others have nothing to do with us".
You might have known,
the lapping waves

of territory,
the almost distant footsteps
of slaves,
and the sugar taste in your mouth.
The stain of things, unexplained
by points of steel and concrete,
spreads; the river rises.
The new bridge across the city
almost touches the water when heavy rain falls.

Connolly

The sun falls through the station
the rolling stock and smoke
Feathers in the drain cling
to the shadows of small dead birds
cast from the roof
over platform no. 1
and someone's first kiss goodbye
A stray dog runs the escalator
against the tide of another struggle
from the shopping centre
Tickets dropped by the timetable
cigarette ends and the Coke machine
Black pigeons drinking
from a pool of steam and oil
The revolution and the plaque by the restaurant
The crumbs and the eggshells
The back of the city breathes
the police helicopter light
You cut your steps out in the underpass
Moving like a leaf

she will rise through the Summer
while you wait for insects to change into flowers

Untitled

The heart with no commission lays leveled by the dawn
Words blue with hunger drag across the morning

The morning slow like a station
waiting on the first train to come

The sound of a telephone like an insect in my ear
This shaking hand leaves her skin like a thief

Her lips woken from the twist of night and tempered in the day
like wrought iron gates beggars do not pass

Shadows of the world move in
like a former lover or a ticket inspector

The remains of a song cling like ashes to the wall

This dying moment clawing at the windowsill
This movement of the sun

Faithless bodies pass from ourselves against each other

One more time beneath the make-up and the radio

Dressing in the light thrown from a glass of water
she made me think of days without her

Comedians

.... the moon is neither here nor there,
it hangs between beats of hearts and drum machines;
a cold omen programmed or a beautiful sign revealed.

(That you or I could each be anyone, in spirit or, at least,
in pieces).

The stars flickering outside the bar are amazing balls of light
(or the glitter left attached beneath your eyes).

Either way they are my navigation, my taxi call, my exit sign;
billboards above the street screw along the queue
like the unknown hopeless gropes falling on the road.

... at the end our spirit is not so much to speak of,
perhaps it never was; a passing thought
we checked with our coats.

(Like anything we have, it's suited to what we want).

St. Jude's Poem

Media and prayers have infiltrated your hopelessness.
They do not claim to understand.
They see you standing on burning balconies,
in silence, with your honour in rags beside you.
But you keep close the grace of despair and the comfort
    of priests.
You embrace any cold glass shrine case.
Your honour necessitates petitions of burning cities.

One day you will be torn from it,
in a laneway where death runs like a bull.
Then at least you'll get a rose between your teeth.
And you'll know how to use a flower when the time comes.
It brings me to tears.
You have joy only in what your shadow casts;
and when funerals pass by, you overwhelm me.

The Fountain
(After St. Patrick's)

People return their library books conscientiously
on Saturday morning. I don't know where I am.

A fountain in Eyre Square spews green water,
as if it was meant to. As if you might even believe it.

Although used to blatant displays of this nature,
it still upsets you. Read on a wall, "BEAUTY

IS ON THE INSIDE". The small print unclear.

Like a foreigner, or a spy, I conspire to spot my own kind.
Neither of us really care. Or say anything much about it.
(At least here they know how to contain a shopping centre).

Like any illegal worth his salt, found a good dark end
at the bar, just light enough to establish
the girls are pretty sitting on the wounded knee of America.

Lost off High Street, the optimism of a small city strikes me
when the sunrise and Hare Krishna chants collide.

I can still say only what I am not. Mumbling Montale,
that one phrase in Italian. Like any good forgetful night,

find a friend who talks more than you. Even *as Gaeilge*;
you can pretend to listen. You might even believe it yourself,

when you tell people if you lived where they did
you would also return your library books on time,

not read the small print; optimistically watch the sunrise
                              drown itself in green.

33

Galway Road (into Dublin)

I.

With this stillness, the stone walls
like borders, despite the light on your face
there is nothing you can declare.

As if our faith could have worsened
since I saw you last. As if
the changes mean that much.

Careless and ancient, like a myth,
you step into view; spitting shadows from your mouth.

Out from behind the barricades
you look raped and haunted.

II.

Now is not the time to find her in the morning,
as you go flushed out by trial and error.

The streets suck you through

the doorways and the rooms.

The glass bank buildings leave us

like whores in the morning after.

Hidden

We have not found each other yet.
We're both of us well hidden from the other.
We're hidden by our friends and hidden in the mirror.
Hidden in the doorways and hidden in these lines.
We're hidden beneath the laws of sex and economics.
Hidden by each lonely thing we do for money.
Hidden by weddings, functions and death.
We're hidden by design and by accident.
Hidden in the calendars and hidden in the books.
Tied to the bars, the corridors and rooms.
Hidden on the tenth floor and hidden by the rosebush.
We're hidden at birth, in hope and parades.
Hidden in the telephones, the traffic and stations.
Hidden when we meet by the faces of strangers.

Smithfield

It has been beaten into shape;
we find ourselves drinking
to the banging of bodhrans
and the rattle of banjos.
(As if it was meant to be
like this long ago).
The smell of fruit and horseshit
mixed with perfumed paper
weaves through a silent market.
It spreads from the middle out
to the edge, selling Irish Things,
that would not be claimed
in any lost and found.
A Celtic cross on a bog muck base,
a jacket made of dried up grass
and a twisted woman hammered
out of bronze.
(The word "*Gaeilge*" here and there,
for authenticity).
It has been beaten into shape,
like the watchtower in the village,
fortified; and the price goes up,
another level of things to protect.

Lobby

There are jackboots in the hallway
you hear them from the rooms
where burdens are handed out
from those without faces
to those without names

There are hearts beating in the porches
or they hang around tables
in the hope they may be claimed
clutched for a while like small change
Voices slide behind the doors

like gas they mark the days
when your secrets will be uncovered
by the march of ultraviolet
Decoded and dismembered
Passed from desk to file

Women in White

Women in white glide down the stairs
like slow sheets of ice.
They come and whisper beside me,
the names of other people I should have loved.

Women in white drift through the room,
like news from Buenos Aires.
For the memory of something else,
they check the fingerprints on their breasts.

For the mistakes I made yesterday
they make me drink straight from their lips.
Women in white come and lie beside me,
whisper the names of others they have treated kindly.

Taxi

Waiting on a taxi
we pick our way through
rose bushes,

nursing wounds
we asked of each other.
Small birds trapped;

the squall of dust
dark blood
and guns. Rooted

like targets in a beam.

The beating of a wing
opens
along the cherry trees.

Black State Cars

I ruined the quiet correspondence
you maintained throughout
the flagwaving and the flames,
the distance to the unmarked grave.
I went to touch you
and the swans scream me down.
There has been no revolution;
the trains still run,
the factories sound the hour
and the sky is still torn from the sun.
Something here has changed.
Since I kissed you in an alleyway,
mistook the miracle mile
and stumbled on frightened shrines.
The police force cling to black state cars.
A warm July breeze. Our ghost
on the tram lays claim to a shadow.

By the church where you cried
I saw the sun bleed to death and tried
to tell of this. I took the silence you
left and the swans screamed me down.
Their feathers left ripples between us.
The moon put a measure on my failure.

The Widow

The widow prays outside the church
for strength to carry on her husband's
work. The family gather to push
for the proper execution of the will.
They move against each other like armies
or chambers of representation.
The draughtsman-ship of grieving and
the gilded chess set of hearts invoked;
more than bodies are buried in the ground.

From behind the curtain of music and smoke,
the skeleton of politics and the shadow of remorse
show themselves like clouds of light,
not even enough to illuminate a course
of action between them. These schemes,
these greater things; the acceptance of death
or, at least, of terrible illness.

These schemes, these greater things, we
cannot contend with even as one. We
come together like tiny balls of fire,
(not even enough to light a course or
departure between us). We fracture
ourselves for economics, inherit methods
of acceptance; words to explain away
other words. History is painted
in new colours, tagged like a swan
or a dolphin. Passed into portrait
and examined for faults when our eyes grow weak;
when we cannot move
without a torch or guiding hand.

The Heiress

The proud heiress shows herself again, beneath the flags,
between the flames, of enterprising nations.
All the president's cars roll down twelve avenues;
you lumber through the city with swallow's tails,
through worn out stones past the Urchins and cheap
    bracelet stores.
Imagine the lady deserves a gift of some sort,
some souvenir you'll carry to show you thought of her.
(A leather bound prayer book or Creole voodoo doll).
Rain falls through the cathedral while she sleeps, and the
    morning stalls.
You want to tell the park attendant,
who grows roses in the financial district,
of the wheelings and dealings, of the lazy smell of death.
But she tore sunlight to her lips,
held the day fixed against her breast
and left you at the station kicking dirt from your shoe.
Delayed at the subway by the words of Jesus Christ
begging for cigarettes, and the sound of an organ grinder
belting out a living, filtered through to unborn children,
undertakers and flower selling women.
Phone sex conversations and rumours of unrest
skirt the business lunches and bazaars,
she drags you down Sebastopol,
steel-eyed but dressed like a swan.
Strip club members beat their bones with rotting fish;
another two-backed monster falls from the Turkish curtains.
You think of her aligned to feathers and French cinema posters,
naked in a shower scene; but that's not where she is.
The proud heiress shows herself again,
beneath the flag, between the flames of enterprising nations,
in the songs of blood drying on a thorn bush,
the trail of Autumn, the city fleeced;

the shadow falling across your mother's face.
You fall into a house you know you've seen before;
the proud heiress at the end of the hall
laughing at a monument to World War I.
Crowded in a room of ornaments and reliefs,
her congregation of screaming doves, wounded dogs,
and investigators of states woo her with arrangements
of sanguine tangoes, tiger lilies and corpses.

Perversion at the Winding Stair
Bookshop & Café

Three floors above the Ha'penny Bridge
The wind off the Liffey howling like new religion
    through the streets
A prophet in a raincoat holds court in Russian
A jazz guitar tunes every napkin to poetry
The Dutch tourist keeps time with his pen on the ashtray
A French girl might be sketching me
I do my best to look across the room capable of something

I realise I have no favourite woman and no mother tongue

Speaking the language of short affairs and civic buildings
Proposed afternoons Che Geuvara credit cards

I miss the alcoholics
The five in the morning bullshit
Thinking now of a woman's dry oligarchy
The order of her heart
The meritocracy of her sex

Victory Park / Park Pobedy

for Lanichka

In this room I feel we are a temporary thing
already outpaced by the fireworks and parades
With millions of others we evaporate daily
steam up through the grates to buildings and machines
Moving slowly through the underpass
steps echo
like the sound
of a poorly strung guitar
I hear the same music everywhere
from the drunken band in the old dark square
to the click and squeak of the secretary's heels

One door becomes another
voices float across the landings;
calling to their women or howling at the moon
On Victory Park the flags have changed again
You are a stranger surrounded by parking spaces
and restaurant tables
the conversation turns
to who now holds the microphone
In a karaoke bar everyone has the chance
to show the world they could have made it

The Red Star still shines at night
on top of Leningradski Station
The soldiers wear it too
like the mothers of the dead
they go on begging for change
None of them have turned into their heroes yet

The flowers in the corner will not tease you again
you touched them once and they turned to dust
At last you have swept the eyelashes from the pillow
and wiped her makeup from the sheets

You have taken the hairpin from under the bed
wiped it clean and given it to someone else
who asked no questions (tied back her hair)
Slipped from her clothes to the floor
The signs of a state that is no more run along the road
8th of March Catherine Wheels collapse in the sky
A piano across the courtyard (some young widow)
The cars and flowers will soon emerge from the snow

From a woman you gathered the memory of love
sitting on the floorboards with the others
waiting for a wind to come in off the sea
and reach you mid-continent primed like a bomb

From the underpass to the street we move like steam
On Victory Park the flags have changed
You did not notice
the fireworks final dance
or the yellow light dimmed down the street
The new religion is a lot like the old
(she ties back her hair
and arranges her clothes)
Last year's dirt lodged on the window ledge
she complains her feet are cold
Summer shoes soaked in melting snow

End of December

I.

Swans press their beaks against the ice
and pick at strands of grass and weed,
scavenging a meal this morning.
The ghosts of cars pass;
evening hangs from a tree.
(It's a long way back,
from the cold tips of your fingers
stretched beneath the covers
for words that would make our heads turn).
It's a long way back
now your words cling to everything.

II.

The flowers you planted on the balcony
are dead since October,
their colour still, cracked and frozen.
(To the sound of invisible freight trains,
fireworks in December
find their way across the tracks,
like words slipped from mouths
that have nothing left to say.
Small birds pick at eggs blown from the drain;
winged cannibals,
turn and stride across the sky
like unanswerable prayers).

III.

Short skirts float by the window,
eyes tired of looking out for others
blink across the street.
Outside of love,
your ambassadors have fallen
crushed beneath the wheels.
Their cries like hearts
that fade from fire into music.

The Hand

Speaking of a nature we could not imagine
I say to you, your skin
will never be party to anything brutal.
(I, on the other hand,
have shaken off all saintly beginnings
in favour of elevator doors
and crumpled sheets.
Control yourself. We will warm to these).
Control yourself, we have a hand
in the future.
Though we are pieces sprinkled on a battlefield,
though we curse and scatter ourselves
across the bathroom floor,
we carefully map where the other lands
(and determine, loosely, borders);
we guide the missiles, we sound the warning
then spy for the other side.

Speaking of a nature no-one could imagine,
five floors up there is only your skin.
Control yourself, we will warm to these things,
balance ourselves for what is to come;   our future
like a cuckold, hanging strangled from the moon.
Speaking of this, your thighs
in the dark make uneasy targets
for one who has no halo, for one without wings.

The Lantern

She carries her lantern like a child through the hallways,
and shines a light in your eyes to make her body a secret.
She rings a bell of porcelain at a station on the plains.
You stumble like a shadow across the mountains.
There is still no duty in anything here but time
called, you've remained to bleed a little.

Wings unveiled she moves above the police surveillance.
The swans block your way. Even the whores scream
from the balcony, shout down the Summer on a bridge
of starving Christmas trees. The stars bow out drunk
    but like targets.
You go along the street and swear in the name of Jesus Christ.
Try another poison. The new one has worn off.

She keeps to herself the taste of belief. You bite your tongue
on the Host and wash it through with alcohol. She stops
for confession at a railway station waiting room.
You haul the moon out of the river, endeavour to become
the accomplice of your shadow and make up the days,
the distance between you.

Flowers on Clarendon Street

Step past the river—
wide with tears
and exhausted roses.
Drawn beneath the stars
and billboard advertisements,
the streets are dark marine.
Falling through headlamps,
horns howl from the corner
to the bridge where love has jumped.
Sparrow's wings drag the night
through screaming;
through violins and feathers,
through the metres of regret.
In a market-place of bones
hearts choke
on the seeds of themselves.

Your Empire

Serena, you are dragging down the boys.
We've gathered to surrender
all the legendary love affairs
that swelled our hearts to bursting.
We've gathered to surrender
all those legendary lovers
to anyone who'll listen.
To the barman with a wink for every woman you bring
through his door after twelve,
to the free spending tourists held up on the Green,
to the rigours of the taxi rank
and the four-in-the-morning hotdog stall.

You should be happy, you did this without knowing.
Smiled like a school-girl in a blue 5 Mark *kino*
then shook us down in a cheap strip tease show.
Your reputation is a tightrope.

Even so,
you throw flowers angled dangerously against me.

Though your heart is a satellite
your empire has no bounds, (European and violent).
But we have shared moments of geography.
The neon church centre-piece in West Berlin,
speeding across a bridge in Dublin
or moving slowly between Dover and Zeebrugge.
(You were a stone bird perched in each glass forest).
You should be satisfied with the ground you covered.

But,
by the flowers laying on the windowsill,
by the military rags in the market down the street
your Empire moves in; spirited by the river
cold through the evening.

Excerpt from a conversation

".... and said I walk these foreign streets well,
drink just like a local, accepted by the pimps
and refuse collectors. For my love is not just
a five hour flight away.
She rests behind innumerable barricades.
.... my head knows this cold marble curve,
the secret Arabic telephone and the silence
against desire which, somewhere along the line,
captured all of us.
.... Think the coffee's strong, the spirit's too sweet
but sweet still for half wakened dreaming.
and closer than she is to me.
.... the cigarettes are different here,
the street signs, you get used to it,
the morning crawling behind your eyes
.... said like everything, you get used to it".

Paris

Old cities like this waste nothing
They change themselves to become the target
Of new lovers everywhere

Old cities like this fill quickly with the dead
They grow from layer upon layer of ash
Gilded by ghosts

Old cities love nothing
Well used to flowers and broken hearts
Escaping themselves

And old cities waste no time
They break new love affairs like twigs
Every morning

Lord Pembroke

Kavanagh and Greacen had breakfast together
in a lodging house around the corner,
off Pembroke Road. Years ago.
Pembroke Road, these days, finance
and tailored shirt tails.

Move on.

Baggot Street is a tower turned on it's side.
It rolls it's people from doorway to doorway
like loose change. There's a girl in a coffee shop
who I saw once five years ago in a park.
I suppose she's moved on by now.

Strange, I met Greacen last week

and walked by Kavanagh's house this morning.
Now this face from five years ago;
this face I never said two words to.
I can't blame either man for that—

the address I wanted, on Pembroke Street.
My fault, and the aristocracy of course
for mapping out the world and quickly
naming it before they leave.

The Veil

I have not noticed
the flowers of February
cast beneath the snow.

I have not broken
the leaves from the trees;
you make your own way.

Supposed weddings
and funerals pass.
Unknown as they are.

I have not seen
your face withdrawn
from the morning's veil,

drawn the stars to you
nor spared a thought
for your family.

I have not gained
your flesh and your tears,
these hands like smoke

have not touched
your solitude.
Unknown as they are.

Girl from Toronto / Paris Bar

She sits before you outstretched,
untouched like some part of Canada.
New and bilingual, her stillness;
her borders quiver in the wind.

These days that hawk their silence,
the distance left between her
and you in cities where everyone
has been reborn before and the squares

are crowded with secrets.
She tells you about driving
open country to Montreal
in her daddy's 8 litre Continental.

But sounds repeat to you
in crosslines from the network,
the traffic and television;
the days you were stripped from belief

in the weather and your blood.
Her voice and her fingertips
they'll brush you like dust;
her stillness suspects you of everything.

Station

there was a time
I almost forgot the name
the plants that grew up against the wall
receded, like things do
the flowers on the balcony
died facing the light
as the convent of St. Anne's
went up in flames

the pillow arched against the headboard
begins to fall out of place
for the last time
I forget the shape it made
the hand carved candles
that were Adam and Eve
have dissembled themselves
into plastic and wax

the flowers on the balcony
died facing the light
the fragrance in the hallway has changed;
the bare beams of a burnt out roof
blackened cloth more black than before
and tiny altars that will not hear prayers again

Almost Sung

You were so quiet when we walked that night
I could hear every intonation of the church bells.
Your spell woven fine as a spider web;
These were fragile times.
Your lips moved somewhere between
the final peel of metal and the click of your new high heels.

Sniper

There is nothing new in death.
As the year ends the clearing out of things
seems almost halfway decent of Him.
There is nothing new in death,
not the way it falls across various faces,
finds you staring at the embers
of photographs and hair-clips,
or comes to children;
their tiny hearts twisted by it's clammy hands.
There is nothing new in death,
it's expression never changes.
There is nothing new in it's long white legs,
it's flagging mouth or fractured skull.
There is nothing in the prayers,
the things to say or what's supposed to come
that can change it.
There is nothing new in the sniper's sights,
in a line of light broken across
the cold calves of upturned corpses
rising in piles from atrocities.
There is nothing new in death,
the way it's carried through the streets,
decked with black sheets and roses.
There is nothing new,
not even in the wood that holds it,
or the rooms weighed up in fear
where no-one smiles except Him,
who proposes Himself passing over
the clean sheets and pressed pajamas.
There is nothing new in death,
it finds you staring at the fingers
of others whose bones are breaking.
Nothing new

in the clearing out of things.
It seems almost decent;
empty buildings on reclaimed land,
the flight of gulls to die at sea
and children kicking through piles of leaves
lining the road from church to cemetery.

Canal Bridge

I.

She looks like she lives in other people's rooms
Reading gossip from Cosmopolitan
applying her make-up on the bus
Her eyelids green-blue
Her lips have frozen over
(And the canal she passes has frozen too;
swans conduct their escape
like ballerinas sliding
through the hands of strangers)

II.

Clawing at his beard
Re-reading the weather forecast
and the property reports
The man sitting behind
might have fallen in love
moments ago
Extricates himself
from another tangled deal
in the Longford Leader
She alights at the corner before his
Two stops down he bins the news
Soon busy proving himself
with department managers
and marketing meetings
(And the street he passes
has hardened too;
dogs sit in the cold
waiting for someone
to call them home)

III.

Long after one of us does not remember
the little marks we left
or how close we could have got
if we had not seen ourselves
slimming in semi-detached rows
by the remains of Christmas trees
those with pet cats to play with
those who have photographs
they will run their fingers
along their favourite scars
Tripping over wish bones
splintered and light
Long after one of us does not remember
crossing the Royal Canal
I let go your hand for the last time

The Wrecking Yard

A Honda sign hangs
by the side of the road
like an apple waiting to fall
from an old dead tree.
The world is what it always was,
gravity continues drawing to a close.
In a line of airbags, roll-bars and badges
passengers wait
for the right time to come.
Road lamps flower and drift past like planets;
dead machines are lit like stars
outside the wrecking yard.

Basilica

I.

Hard faced St. Peter's
drags the light across;
slowly, the afternoon
makes it like a clock.

Minutes torn
from the walls
of monuments
I'd sworn I forgot.

II.

Driving through Cassino,
the smell of tanks and rain;
the grotto at Sora lightly policed
by a boy with a melting cone.

III.

Up the mountain in a Fiat from Atina,
a valley worn into the sky;
barely spare a breath,
trace my steps through the street.
Sunlight at that altitude,
consumed by the trees.

IV.

The junction at Colosseo,
the bubbling tar of Mussolini's roads;
the Emperor's new clothes
slowly drag the light across
fingerprints on marble walls.
I'm caught
drunk on Peroni,
bought from a stall,
in a swarm of yellow
ribboned teenage pilgrims.

My mother would think
I'm no-one's son at all.

V.

Walking through the hallways of her government.
I bought nothing Imperial,
—Jubilee Rosary beads.

Stepped from the last moment of my religion
like a clerk
winding up a file
stamping out the end of his duty,
his approval on the ruins.
A woman I'd been watching
for a while,
at least
the time it took
a pearl of sweat to move
from her lips
to her high burlesque chest.

VI.

A dead cat in the wolf's lair,
a shadow twitching behind it,
rarified. Six o'clock,
a deck chair at Ostia.

At least you saw the sharp end
of a real Roman road.

VII.

A woman flung her body
hard against the bricks,
above the orders
of the Throne.
A pearl of sweat running
down her chest,
her little prayer in Spanish;
a small boy crying
by the wall of a church
you swore you forgot.

Prospekt Mira

Sometimes when it rains
I hear the sound of your fingers
tapping against the glass.
I do not remember then
someday it will seem
as if we never met

and the pretty blonde whores
that wander through the supermarket
will remind me of someone else.
Sometimes when it rains,
I forget the distance between us.
In the damp and heat
I neglect the simple truths of geography;

the continents, the gulfs and ravines.
We sit at different tables

but sometimes when I eat alone
I forget you are in love
with someone I don't even know,
and imagine, in certain restaurants,
you would like this place.
But sometimes when it rains,
I hear your voice

like a hypnotist
binding all your spells together,
to make me believe
you no longer love me.

Passage

Everyday
you let it go by
something happens.
A cup
develops rings,
a table
draws dust.
Everyday
you let it go by
a peach or
a carton of milk goes off.
Everyday
you pass yourself
in the mirror,
then,
you stop that
and catch a look
here and there;
in a glass doorway
or the black heart
of a television.
Everyday
you let it go
a few thousand,
(at least), die
in a violent way.
A small percentage
of your belongings
depreciate
in line
with some given
economic index.
Everyday

you let it go by
something happens;
the rope frays
as does your trouser leg.
Everyday
something crawls
into the world
and gives itself a name,
fumbles for change
and the best way
to recline
against the light.
Everyday
you let it pass
something grows
of it's own accord.
Sometimes
it happens
there is also rain.